AIKMAN

MIND, BODY & SOUL

Text by Troy Aikman
Photography by Marc Serota
Edited by Elise Krige Glading

Photography & Picture Editor:
Marc Serota

Editor & Project Coordinator:
Elise Krige Glading

Designed & Produced by:
Rare Air
1711 N. Paulina
Chicago, IL 60622
773.342.5180

Designed by:
John Vieceli & Seth Guge

Published by:
EGI Productions Inc.
3901 South Ocean Drive Suite16L
Hollywood, FL 33019
954.455.1292

EGI Productions: Sales & Marketing
Scott Goldman

Distributed by:
Benchmark Press.
A Division of Triumph Books
601 South LaSalle Street
Chicago, IL 60605
312.939.3330

Special Thanks
Charlyn Aikman & The Aikman Family

Thanks:
At AIKMAN ENTERPRISES:

Carol Hitt

Fred Schreyer at Intersport Management
522 SW 5th Avenue, #1250 Portland, OR 97204

Howard Schwartz, Dan LeClair, Dan Marino and Mr. M Senior, Ralph Stringer,
Foley's Department Stores, John Elway. MET-Rx, Beth & Colin Braley, Midwestern State University,
The Fort Worth Star Telegram, Cool River Cafe, Irving,TX; Juliana Fisher, Canon EOS cameras.

At The DALLAS COWBOYS FOOTBALL ORGANIZATION:
Jerry Jones and the Cowboys organization, Rich Dalrymple, Brett Daniels, Rhonda Worthey, Bruce Hardy
at Texas Stadium, Joe Avezzano, Bucky Buchanan and the entire Cowboys training staff.

At SAM'S CLUB:
Donna Owens and Sharon Kidd

At KODAK:
Tim McCabe

At BENCHMARK:
Mitch Rogatz, Peter Balis, Laura Moeller, Bill Swanson & Heather Hotaling

At RARE AIR:
Mark Vancil, Jim Forni and John "the genius" Vieceli

At the NFL:
Pete Abitante & Jim Saccomano

COOK CHILDREN'S MEDICAL CENTER

With loving thoughts of: Ben Krige, Irma Weiner and Fran Greene

EGI Books may be purchased for educational, business or
sales promotional use. Send inquires to Sales and Marketing,
EGI 3901 South Ocean Drive Suite 161 Hollywood, Florida
33019. First Edition 1998.

Table of Contents

Chapter 1 Mind pg.8

Chapter 2 Body pg.42

Chapter 3 Soul pg.92

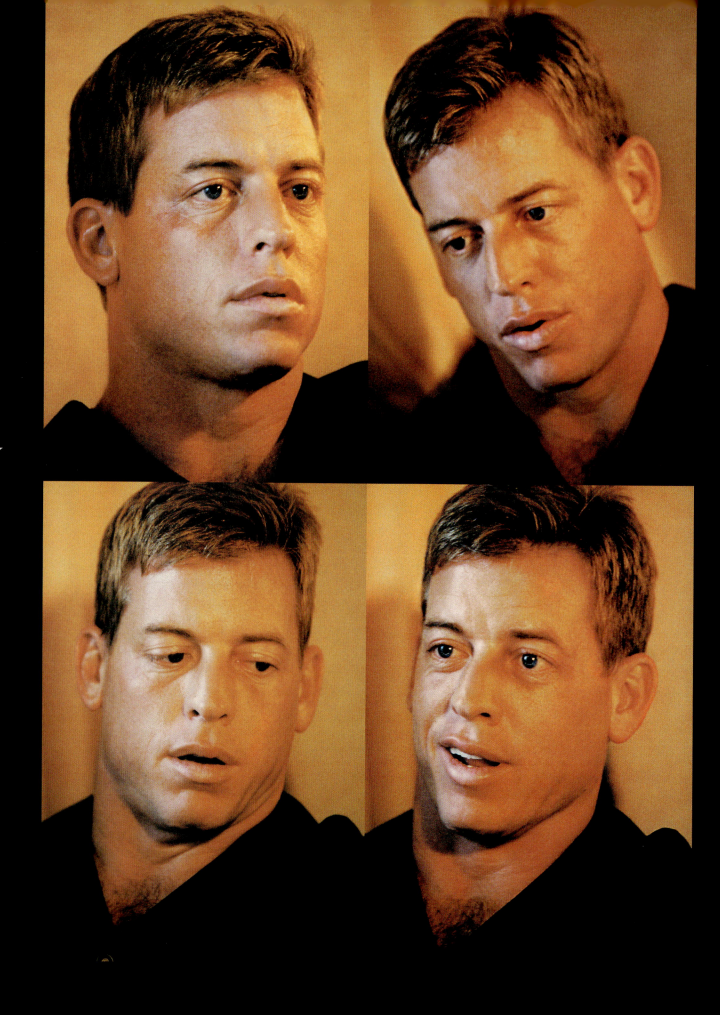

As far back as I can remember,
I always loved sports and dreamed of
being a professional athlete. I was born
on November 21, 1966, in
West Covina, California.

Though I had a mild form of club foot as an infant, I always had a ball in my hands growing up and I loved playing sports with my friends. My two older sisters, Terri and Tammy, were cheerleaders, so I was exposed to sports before I was at an age where I could participate in them. I really just fell in love with sports. I began playing contact football, baseball and basketball when I was eight. All I wanted to be was a professional athlete. When people asked me what I wanted to do when I grew up, I'd tell them I wanted to be an athlete. I was fortunate I was able to fulfill that dream. I guess I was born to be an athlete. It is important to have dreams and goals. If you dream, you might as well dream big. I used to visualize my dreams. I realized I had to make myself the best player I could be, but I never got too far ahead of myself. I realized that in order to ultimately get what I wanted, there were certain steps that had to be taken. First, I had to make the high school team, then college, then pro-they all build on one another.

In California, my friends and I used to play sports, in all seasons. In summer we would be out in the park playing baseball, football, pick-up games or over-the-line. We also played basketball in the gym, or in the outdoor parks. Everything we did revolved around athletics. When I was 12 my family moved from California to a home about seven miles outside of Henryetta, Oklahoma. It had a population of about 6,500 at the time. It's less than that now. In the beginning, it was difficult to adjust to life in a rural area. I was used to riding my bicycle wherever I wanted to go in California. With the dirt roads, I wasn't able to do that anymore and I really missed my friends. It was frustrating, but I grew to like the closeness of the community in Henryetta and its support of the kids. I identified with the people so well, that type of lifestyle. I learned to appreciate the hard-working, yet laid-back, easy-going people. The values they share in small communities — I enjoyed everything about growing up in a small town in rural America. It turned out to be a very good experience for me and helped shape my attitude toward life.

I've experienced many changes in my life and I think, like most people, I have a bit of resistance to change. But I've learned over the years that some of the best things that have happened in my life were a result of change. Some of the things that I have resisted the most, have turned out to be the most rewarding. I'm still, like everyone, resistant to it, but I try to maintain optimism about it, knowing that a lot of good can come from change.

When I was in 8th grade I played tight end and full-back, but other than that I played quarterback every year. I preferred that. I played middle linebacker and safety on defense when I was growing up and I guess if I wasn't playing quarterback today, I probably would want to play linebacker on defense.

I never look back and think, what if? Everyone makes decisions about different things, and some of the decisions I've made have been really good ones, and some have not been good. But I've never looked back and thought how my life could have been different. In 1984 the New York Mets were interested in drafting me, but I made a choice to play college football instead and I don't look back and wonder what my life would have been like if I had chosen a professional baseball career instead.

In high school I played football, center in basketball and shortstop or pitcher on the baseball team. Football, however, became my favorite sport and I set a goal to play in college. After high school I decided to play football at the University of Oklahoma and was a management information systems major there. I really enjoyed studying business, finance and marketing and was just getting into my major, but my college football debut was disappointing. Injuries to quarterbacks ahead of me in 1984 pushed me into the starting job as a freshman before I was ready. Oklahoma entered the 1985 season rated No 1. in the country. The pressure was on. We won our first three games before facing Jimmy Johnson's Miami team. I started hot, but moments later my season came to a painful end when two Hurricanes tackled me. I landed on my left leg and broke my ankle. Quarterback Jamelle Holieway stepped in and led the team to a national title. Coach Barry Switzer went back to running the wishbone offense and I soon realized that if I stayed with the Sooners there was a good chance I'd be riding the bench my last two years in college. That definitely would have hurt my development as a quarterback.

I was also ready to go back to California, so I transferred to UCLA. UCLA did not have a business school at the time, which really surprised me. The only thing it had that would have enabled me to apply my credits was sociology, which is a broad major. So I majored in sociology at UCLA.

Over the years I've tried to learn something from the disappointments that I've had in my life. I usually come to the conclusion that I must work harder. Despite all our wins, we lost the two most important games. Both years we were knocked out of the race for the Rose Bowl by losses to cross-city rival USC. I had to learn to overcome the disappointment of those defeats and to move along. I enjoyed playing for the Bruins, and I particularly enjoyed playing in the Aloha and Cotton Bowl games. In the 1987 Aloha Bowl Emmitt Smith, who was a Gator running back, and I were named co-MVPs. I played my last college game in Dallas at the Cotton Bowl in 1989, where we beat Arkansas 17-3, and where I was named MVP of the game. That whole period was really strange. It was fun, but it was also nerve-wracking. I wanted to do well in the Cotton Bowl, I guess because I felt deep down that I would be playing in Dallas. It was important for me to come out and play well and at least give the people in Dallas some kind of hope that I'd be a good player for the city.

I'm more focused on the field than off the field. But that doesn't imply that I'm unfocused in life — I'm pretty determined as far as what I want to do, and how I want things to be done. I pretty much stick to it — be it in business, family matters, health, hobbies, charity involvement or any other area of my life. I think I'm sort of a different personality on the field than off the field. I'm much more demanding on

the field and a perfectionist on myself. I'm so demanding of myself on the field that I'm exhausted by the time that I get off. I'm not nearly as intense about things off the field. I find that when I focus on the task at hand and concentrate on doing my job, my worries subside. During dark days of losses, injuries and recoveries, I keep my focus and have faith that things will change. When my back's against the wall I'm an

optimist, but I tend to be more realistic in my views. One way or the other, it has been helpful for me, not to get too high when things are going well, and not to get too low when things are going bad. Although I admit to having a tougher time getting over the loses, I realize that there are ups and downs and you have to deal with them and keep going.

My college coach, Terry Donahue, used to tell me that

things are never as bad as you think they are, and they're never as good as you think they are.

That is so true, not only in football, but in life.
As soon as things are going great, then something happens that makes you realize
that things were not really quite that good, and the other way around.

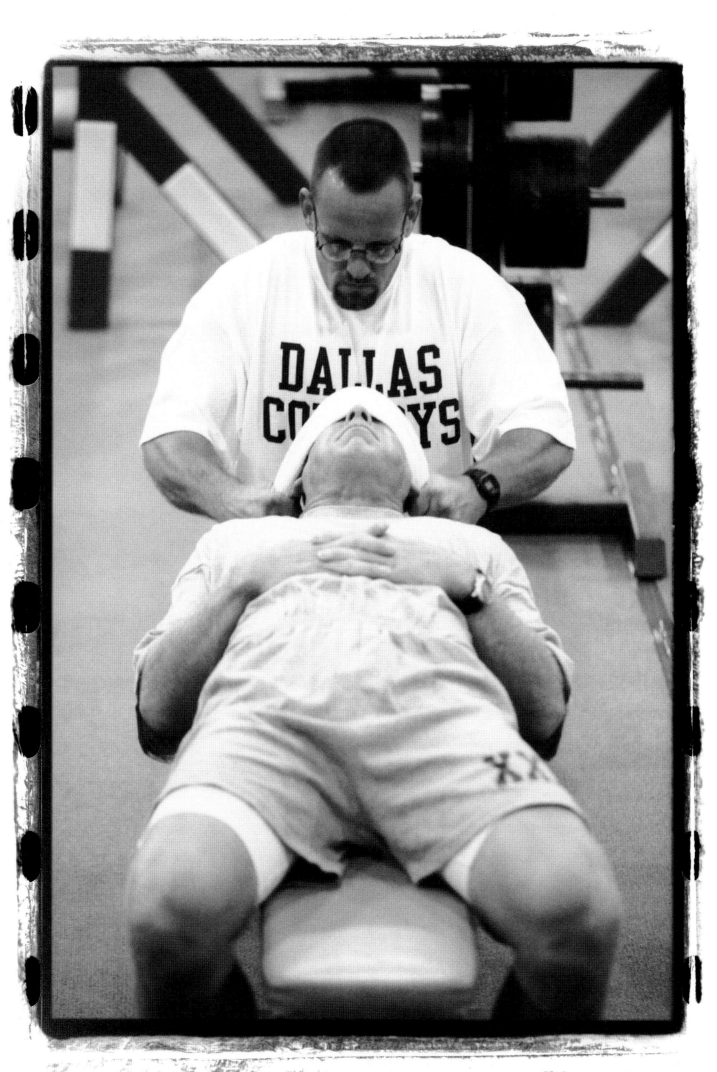

I mentally prepare for games by spending a lot of hours during the week watching film. It also helps me mentally to keep focused by staying in physical shape. I do a lot of running and I feel it helps me to mentally stay in shape. It clears my mind. My game preparations do not change much from week to week. As the game gets closer I tend to get more and more focused mentally. The day before the game I tend to block everybody and everything out. So about 24 hours before the game it's very difficult for me to think of anything other than the game. I have certain routines that I go through on game day as well.

It never has been hard for me to motivate myself. I don't have to go through anything special to get motivated. I've always been a very driven person, who wants to accomplish things, and be successful. It just kind of comes naturally to me. I don't have to talk to myself to get motivated. I think a lot of it has to do with my

upbringing and my father. My father was a very driven guy and very hard-nosed, and that kind of rubbed off on me. My mom is one of the nicest people I know and she was gentle, but firm, raising me. She instilled strong values in me and always encouraged me. My parents were my role models as I grew up.

I exercise my mind by reading. I like reading autobiographies and real life stories, things that actually happened and that I can learn something from as opposed to fictional stories. Early in my professional football career in Dallas I read Terry Bradshaw's autobiography and that really helped me, realizing that other quarterbacks struggle too, and how he dealt with defeats and victories. I've enjoyed reading the autobiographies of Larry Bird, Norman Brinker, Ross Perot and others. It is not always just about athletes. I'm interested in a lot of different things in life and I like to read about a variety of subjects. Most of the time they are not sports related.

I think there are some athletes who can depend a great deal on just their physical skills.
They don't have to spend a lot of time actually studying their opponent, or studying what they are supposed to be doing.
They get away a lot with their athletic ability.

I feel like I have some real God-given talents,
but I think for the most part
it has been hard work that has gotten me where I am.

Being a student of the game

is something that I take a great deal of pride in,
knowing exactly what my assignments are,
and what the game plans are.

For quarterbacks in particular it is important to do that. I spend a lot of time watching film, studying game plans and
studying tendencies of opponents, just so mentally I can be as prepared as I can possibly be. We watch our practice tapes at
training camp, but during the season is when we really study a lot of film of the opponent.

We have scripted plays in the past, the first 15 opening plays, or so. Some teams take it further than that. Some teams do more, others less. I don't know whether we will be doing that this year or what the approach will be, with Chan Gailey as the new head coach and offensive coordinator. We have about 80 different plays at our disposal. When we go into a season we'll have our standard plays that we would put in every week, but then depending on who we're playing we spend a lot of time coming up with new ideas, different wrinkles, things that this opponent hasn't seen yet, just to allow us the chance to make some big plays. It does tend to put them on their heels a bit and catch them off guard.

I must say that I try to master the mental game, by demanding control in the huddle and consistently trying to make intelligent decisions.

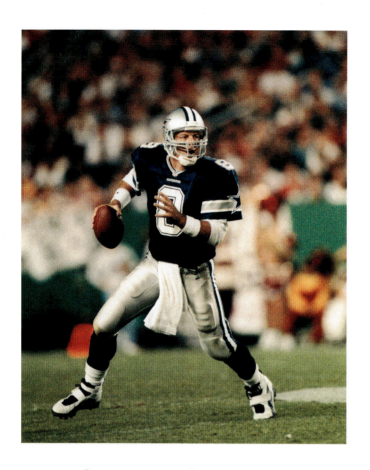 

For the quarterback on passing plays, we read the defense by watching the safeties at the snap of the ball. The safeties will tell you what the coverages are. That's what we mean by reading the defense, it is looking at keys that indicate to you what type of

coverage there is and where the different defenders are expected to go. Once you know that, you know where they are vulnerable within those coverages. Those are the areas we try to exploit. As a quarterback those are the areas that you would try to get the ball into.

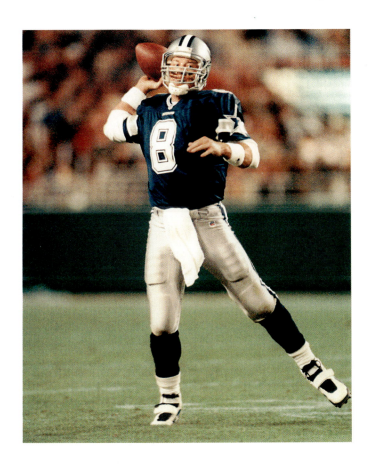

We just put in a new system,
but the key to our success is the ability
to maintain balance offensively.

We feel that we are
at our best when we are
running and throwing
the ball effectively.

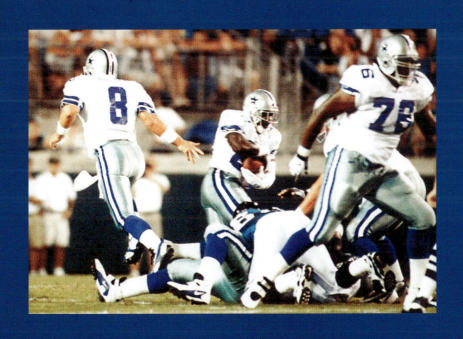

We are not a one-dimensional team.
If we can do both, then that is when we are going
to be at our best. We have done that in the past and
that is why we have had the success we have had.
We will have to stay focused mentally.
When we struggle it is more a lack of
concentration than anything else.

A strong defense is extremely important and I've been fortunate we've had that in Dallas. If you have a good defense you give the offense more opportunities to score. Turnovers give the team good offensive field position. There is no question about it —

a good defense makes for a good offense.

There is not really a specific offensive philosophy that I favor. I believe in doing whatever your personnel allows you to do. Ultimately and optimally you would like to be able to do what we've done in the past, to run the ball and throw it. My philosophy is such that if personnel dictates that you do something else, well then you do that. You do not get so tied up in your own philosophy that you fail to realize what's best for the team.

Football is like a big chess game. You are always anticipating the other guy's move and what he might do. Then you do something a little bit differently, you never want to get too predictable. It's certainly a very physical, violent game, but what really separates teams and athletes is the mental

aspect of it. Especially at this level, the talent is not that much different, but it is who is able to execute, who is able to avoid the mental breakdowns. I think so much of the game is played from the shoulders up.

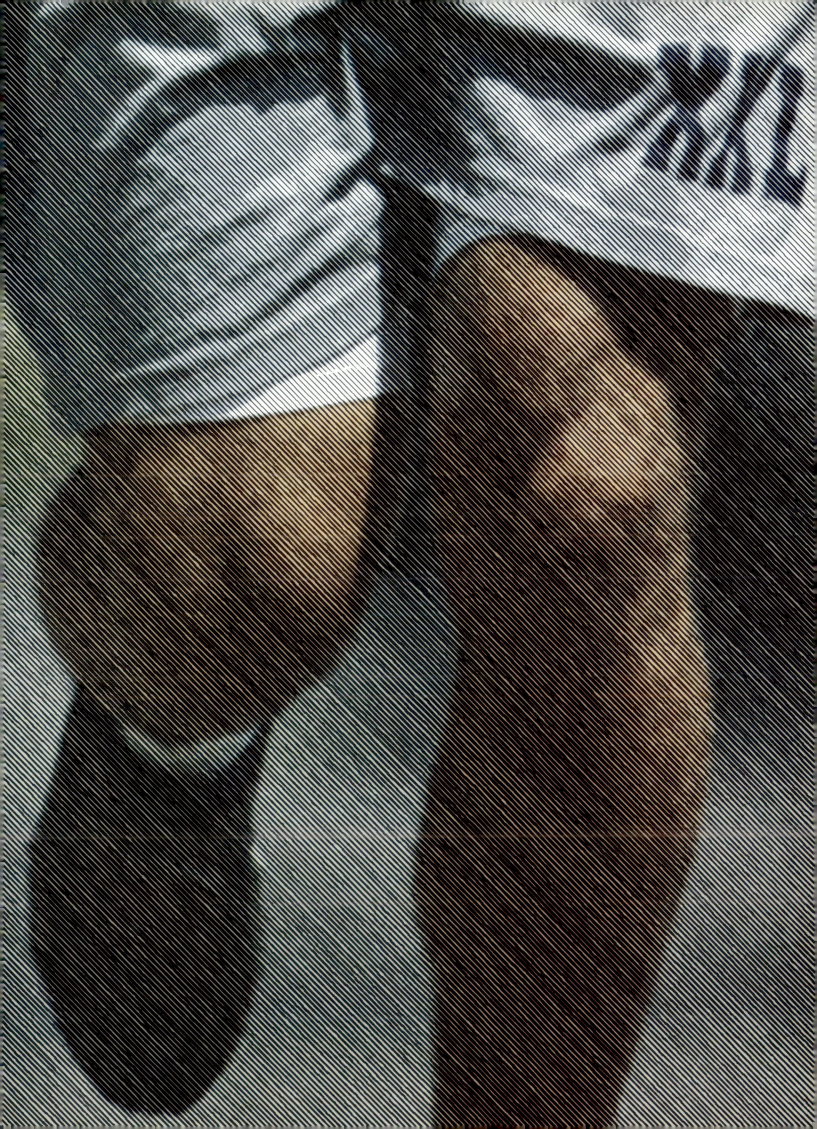

Chapter 2

I spend a lot of time throwing balls, but I think that my passing skill is really a natural ability. I'm a fairly accurate passer and that just comes pretty naturally. I didn't spend a lot of time working on being accurate, it just kind of happened. Passing accuracy is real important in having any degree of success as a quarterback. I'm compact in the way that I throw the ball and that probably developed from playing baseball. A quick release also helps you because reaction time for the defender becomes so much less.

Ten years of playing the game professionally, you start seeing things a little better, your field vision improves, and little keys in the defenders are more noticeable. It's very difficult to see the whole field, but you see indicators in what the defenders will do that allow you to know that somebody is open. So you react on that.

After years of playing you start developing an awareness

of what is happening around you. When I really get on a roll throwing the football, I feel I can take control of the game and that I'm going to complete every pass I throw. It's a great feeling.

I've always felt that for me to be at my best, I needed to keep in shape. I've always enjoyed working out. It

served as a tremendous stress release for me. Compared with a lot of quarterbacks, I lift a lot of weights. I lift a great

deal during the off-season, four times a week, and I run almost every day. During the summer I run outside and

during the winter I run on the treadmill inside or use the stairmaster, or something like that. I do that almost every

day. Then, during the season, I lift twice a week. It's not real heavy, it's not to try to establish any strength, it's just

to try to maintain what I already have had from the off-season and help alleviate soreness following games. During

the off-season I work hard at trying to stay in shape, and I think it has helped me. I began extensive running and

cardiovascular exercise about four years ago, and I haven't missed a start since I've started doing this. I've been able to stay healthy and it has helped me to feel better too. At the time when I started running, I also really started watch-

ing my diet. I began using products from MET-Rx and it helped supplement my diet. I started avoiding certain foods

and I became much more diligent in my dietary program. It's not too hard during the off-season to maintain my level

of strength, health and fitness because I'm not taking the physical pounding like I do during the season. You recover

from the previous season, with the lifting and running. What I try to do is to develop some level of strength that will

help carry me through the season. It is real difficult to lift and maintain your strength during the season because you

are so physically tired and sore from the consequences of the game. By the end of the season, you're so physically

worn down, but you try to do as much as you can during the off-season, to allow you to get through the season.

I like the new training facility in Wichita Falls. It is really nice. The locker rooms are spacious, we have more room in the weight room and in the dorms. Of course it's hot, but it's hot in Austin too. I think the environment in Wichita Falls is very good. It is also amazing how well Midwestern State University has treated us, the organization, the players, coaches, fans, and everyone involved. We are very happy with the way they handled the training camp facilities and the fans.

Whatever toughness I have comes from the toughest guy I know – my dad.

He never missed a day of work in his life. At an early age, he demanded a lot from me, and we worked hard. I grew up on a ranch in Henryetta, Oklahoma, where I spent a lot of summers hauling hay and working with my dad in the fields. Watching him and how he pushed me, helped develop my physical and mental toughness. Part of the reason I play the way that I do — without fear of getting tackled — stems from back when I was younger and seeing how my dad worked and how tough he was. I wanted to prove to him that I was tough, too. I think that deep down, I always wanted to prove that I was as tough as he was... And I think that through football I was able to prove that to him. I maintain my competitive edge by remembering my roots.

I have had many bumps and bruises in my career, but I have an ability to recover fairly quickly. The reason for that is probably because my body

rebounds very well. I try to keep a positive attitude and remain focused. I took a lot of hits in my rookie year. I broke my left index finger and missed six weeks. Then, in my first game back, I took one of the hardest hits when a Phoenix Cardinal delivered a crushing blow, that knocked me out for eight

minutes. I also remember the first time we played Philadelphia on Thanksgiving. I walked into the locker room after the game and they X-rayed both shoulders, both knees and one elbow. I thought they were going to put me in a body cast, but I wasn't giving up. A positive attitude and the right diet are so important to help you

recover from injuries. I also have a determination that I will come back — and quickly. That attitude, I believe, accelerates my comeback.

I was really excited when the Dallas Cowboys drafted me in 1989. There were two teams that I wanted to play for when I was coming out of college, one of them was the Dallas Cowboys and the other one was the San Diego Chargers. I was fortunate I got to go to a team I wanted to play for. Most players don't get that chance. Dallas is three hours from where I grew up in Oklahoma, so it was like going home in a sense. It was as close as I could get to where I grew up.

The number 8 doesn't really have any special significance. I was No. 10 all through high school and at Oklahoma I wanted 10, but someone else had it. When I transferred to UCLA I wanted 10, but someone else had it so I just picked 8 and I have been wearing it ever since.

I've been with the Dallas Cowboys for nine full seasons and I can't see myself playing for another team. There are guys who you never would have dreamt would play for other teams, like Joe Montana, but I couldn't ever imagine playing for another team. I'm sure, however, that Joe never thought he'd play anywhere other than San Francisco. My contract is also such that I don't think I'll ever play out my contract to go play for another team.

So, if I do play for another team it would be because I was traded.

I'm proud of our Dallas Cowboys team. It is a strange feeling to play for such a legendary team. I always loved watching the Dallas Cowboys play on TV. One of my favorite players was quarterback Roger Staubach. When I joined the team in 1989, things were very bad, we were 1-15. We didn't look much like America's favorite team then. It was tough but we got it turned around, and four years later in my career, in 1992, we won our first Super Bowl. That's when we really started getting on a roll and playing some really good football, and that's when I first realized exactly what this whole America's Team thing came to mean, and the fan support and what it means to play for the Dallas Cowboys. I'm fortunate because so much of the success that I've enjoyed off the field has been a result of playing for this franchise. A lot of the players who have played before me have made this possible: Roger Staubach, Bob Lilly, and others, they are the ones who created all of this. It's a great feeling to be part of an organization that is regarded so favorably and so strongly.

The number 8 doesn't really have any special significance. I was No. 10 all through high school and at Oklahoma I wanted 10, but someone else had it. When I transferred to UCLA I wanted 10, but someone else had it so I just picked 8, and I have been wearing it ever since.

championships

There really isn't a team that I enjoy beating more than others. Certainly there are teams against which we have bigger rivalries than others, and those games are always fun to win. Obviously the better teams, such as the 49ers are always a challenge. We've had a lot of great games against them and it has been such a great rivalry because of the history of the two franchises. We have also had some great games against the Packers. Those are the games that I tend to remember the most because of what's at stake and what's put on the line. That's why we compete, to play in those big games in the hope you will get a chance over the course of your career to play in a lot of them. I have played in many big games and I hope there's a lot more ahead!

I like everything the playoffs represent. I like the finality of it:

AIKMAN

Troy absorbs the media blitz at the Super Bowl.

Winner takes all, loser goes home. I enjoy the sense of urgency that comes with that.

My first Super Bowl, in particular, stands out in my memory. That whole season was a very special year. We started the 1992 season by beating defending Super Bowl champion Washington and everything started bouncing our way from then on. Playing in the Super Bowl the first time was almost like a dream. They announced my name and I ran out onto the field at the Rose Bowl, and there was a tremendous rush, unlike anything I've ever known. We all started off pretty shaky. We had problems getting lined up, and getting the right plays and running them right. We were all a little nervous, but once we settled down, it became like a normal game. It took me about a quarter and a half before I really came back to earth. I kept my focus on what I needed to do moment by moment. We started moving the ball and our team got into a rhythm. We scored on a touchdown pass in the first quarter to tie it 7-7, and from there everything went our way. Our 52-17 victory ranks as one of the most lopsided in Super Bowl history. That first Super Bowl triumph meant everything to me. A tremendous weight was off my shoulders. No matter what happened, I could say that I took the team to the Super Bowl and won it. For me, winning the Super Bowl was a tremendous natural high that lasted the whole off-season. I don't think you ever really do recapture the fun, the excitement and the innocence of that first Super Bowl season.

The second
Super Bowl in Atlanta was
a big game. Two Super Bowls,
two victories — that was almost too
much to believe after winning just
one game four years before. The
pressure to repeat was tremendous.
The pressure stemmed from the fans,
the media and from ourselves.
We had to overcome a lot of
adversity, and had to stay focused
to do it twice in a row. The year
wasn't as much fun. It was more
of a struggle. But the win
was every bit as satisfying.

XXVIII

Troy Aikman celebrates following the end of Super Bowl XXVIII, January 30 in the Georgia Dome in Atlanta.

The third Super Bowl against Pittsburgh was exciting as well. The team overcame more than the other two Super Bowl teams had. It was a very rewarding feeling and a sense of relief for us. After having won the Super Bowl three times in four years, the team made a place in history. It is something that hadn't been done before so that was very rewarding to all of us. Still, I never have been so happy for a season to be over than that one. Each one of the three Super Bowls has been a little different. The pressure to repeat begins as soon as the victory parade is over. It's a vicious cycle.

There were a lot of good games over the years. Winning percentage is the most meaningful statistic to me. My whole thing always has been about winning games, so it isn't important to me what my game and career statistics are. Jerry Jones pays me a lot of money to go and win football games, he doesn't pay me a lot of money to rack up a lot of yards in a loss. I've never been worried about my place in history.

I always have believed I could play with the best quarterbacks in the league, but at first it was strange being out there on the field against guys I grew up watching, like John Elway and Dan Marino. I don't like to rate myself with other quarterbacks. I don't get tied up in that. There are too many other people in the press who want to make comparisons with other players and evaluations. I just want to go out and help the team win, and win championships.

There is nothing better than achieving a goal and sharing it with the guys with whom you've accomplished it. For 53 guys to come together with one common goal and then to be able to go through a season-accomplish that goal and to celebrate together, I don't think there is a better feeling in the world. I have a lot of close friends on the team and I respect all my teammates. They are extremely important to me. I would like to leave this game feeling as though I had the respect of my teammates, much more so than what any fan or anybody in the press could think of me. These are the guys who see me on a daily basis and it is important to me that I have their respect. You spend a lot of time together and really get to know each other. We each have our own separate lives, but during the season we get to know each other very well because we spend so much time together.

The Dallas Cowboys have a lot of good character guys. Some people may tend to disagree, without having first-hand knowledge. As in any business there are some people who would have some problems, and we have some of those, but that doesn't mean the group is not good. The media is very quick to judge and talk about the bad things. They don't spend a lot of time talking about the good things happening on the team.

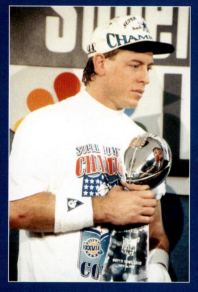

Super Bowl MVP

I am so thankful to be given the opportunity to throw passes to Jay Novacek. People will never understand
how good he was...but I know Jay.

The offensive line for this season is going to be a really good group.

We have Larry Allen at left tackle and Nate Newton at left guard. Clay Shiver will be center. Everett McIver will be our right guard and right tackle will be Erik Williams. It's a very talented group and I think they are going to have a great year. They are going to play hard and are going to win a lot of games. They are playing at a very high level.

The chemistry between me,
Emmitt Smith, Michael Irvin and Daryl
Johnston is great.

We developed in the NFL together. Michael arrived in 1988, Daryl and I followed him in 1989 and Emmitt came in 1990. We've enjoyed our successes along the way with each other, and because of each other. It has been fun playing with them and I hope I will finish my career playing with them. Me, Emmitt, Michael and DJ, we're a very close group. We all are dependent on each other for our team's success and also for our own individual success. We rely on each other. The fact that we all came in together and went through hardships together and got to enjoy our successes together, kept us very close. It has eliminated a lot of the things that have separated some of the good teams, as far as the egos and the petty jealousies are concerned.

Michael and I enjoy a unique relationship. For whatever reason, we always have had a special bond. I love him like a brother. We have the kind of relationship where we know what each other is thinking. He has been through a lot, I know, and he has made some poor decisions he will be the first to admit, but I really think Michael has one of the biggest hearts of anybody I know. I see the compassion and his hard work through the season. I have a lot of admiration for him, for the side of him that I get to see. It is hard for people to understand that sometimes.

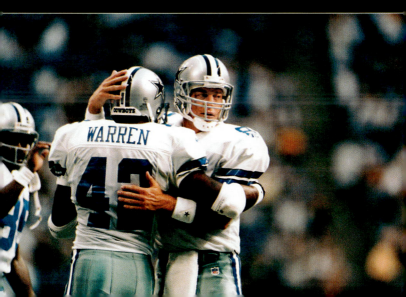

I think teams tend to take on the personalities of their coaches. Coaches Terry Donahue, Jimmy Johnson and Barry Switzer influenced my career in different ways. Terry Donahue was the first head coach who laid the foundation for me in terms of understanding football, how to attack defenses, and the position of the quarterback. Terry was very involved offensively with us while I was in college. I was a transfer student coming in from Oklahoma and UCLA didn't take many transfer students. It was rare for somebody like me to get the opportunity to go play there. He taught me a lot about the game. I had a lot of confidence in my arm when I was at UCLA and Terry used to tell me: "You can't throw a football through a car wash without it getting wet, so stop trying." I used to think that if I wanted to throw a ball somewhere I was going to throw it. I might have had too much confidence in my ability to throw and Terry really stressed the importance of ball security.

Jimmy Johnson and I had a good relationship. I guess it's safe to say that it started off kind of rocky, but then, as we got to understand and to know each other, we were a lot alike. We understood each other's commitment to winning. Through that we developed a friendship and by the time he left we were good friends. We both joined the Cowboys with something to prove. There were many critics who didn't think we could win an NFL championship. Jimmy had success as a college coach, but, at the time, few college coaches had much success in the NFL. He felt that he had something to prove. Once we won that first Super Bowl it took a tremendous burden off both of us so it was a great feeling celebrating the victory together.

I'm very excited about Chan Gailey being hired as head coach for the Cowboys. He certainly has proven himself as an offensive mind in the NFL. He has been associated with some very good offensive football teams over his 10 years spent as an NFL assistant and he has been to the Super Bowl four times. Of course, we're hoping to increase that number!

Over the past few years with the Steelers, he has helped produce one of the top offenses in the game. People he has worked with, such as Dan Reeves, Bill Cowher and Mike Shanahan, all rave about him, so I'm looking forward to working with him. Everything I have heard about Gailey is favorable. I think he will give us a tremendous sense of direction.

Jerry Jones and I have been through a lot together. I was the first player he drafted and signed. My relationship with Jerry and my role in the team has evolved over the years that I've been with the Cowboys. I have got a lot of respect for Jerry as a businessman and as an owner. Jerry is more committed to winning, than he is to making money. As a player you can't ask for anything more than that.

Ultimately, I'm judged on how many games we win and lose. Jerry always has been very upfront and honest with me and always has treated me fairly. He is dedicated to the team and that's the best thing we can ask for. I appreciate him and the relationship we have.

This season the organization is going through its most change in nine years, since Jimmy Johnson took over in 1989. When Barry Switzer came in, most of his assistants were still here, we still practiced the way we had before. There really wasn't that much change in the overall scheme of things with the exception of head coach. We still ran the same offense and defense. Now we have a coach who has different ideas, different practice structure, different ways he wants to do things, and there is tremendous change going on within our organization, I think that brings enthusiasm.

We have great fans. They are extremely loyal. We have a fan base that started many years ago, back in the '70s, with the history of the Cowboys and the success with players such as Staubach and his generation of players. When I first joined the Cowboys, we weren't very good. But we still had a surprising number of fans that would come to hotels on the road. Though not nearly as many as we have had since we started having success. Still, there are some real die-hard fans. The fan loyalty of the Cowboys tends to be passed down from generation to generation. I run into a lot of people who are big fans of the Cowboys because their parents were Cowboy fans. They grew up watching the Cowboys and have become perpetual fans.

I prefer signing autographs for kids because, for the most part, they want it for the right reasons — they are big fans. That's not to say there are no genuine adult fans. I just think the whole autograph thing has taken a different turn from when I was a kid. Now it's such a big industry. It has taken away a bit from giving autographs. You hear people talking about how much autographs are worth and how much money they can get for so-and-so's autograph. When I was young, number one, you didn't get a lot of autographs, and when you did, it was because it was your favorite player's autograph and you kept it. Nowadays I realize that, unfortunately, I can't give everyone an autograph who wants one. I just don't have the time to do that, so I try to lean towards the children. It is a great feeling for us to see the look on a kid's face when it is really meaningful to them and it is something they've wanted for a long time.

Because of the fans,
the rich history and the success
of the team, we have a definite home
field advantage at

Texas Stadium.

It is a relatively small stadium
compared to others.
It holds about 65,000 people,
so it's a relatively intimate
setting, and I like that.
I also enjoy playing in warm
climates on natural grass fields.
So I've always enjoyed playing at
Sun Devil Stadium in Tempe
and in Miami.

I have a pretty good relationship with
the media locally and nationally. I've enjoyed
the relationship for the most part that I've
had with the press. I have gotten to know
a lot of the personalities nationally that have
become very close friends of mine. Pat
Summerall and I had a television show
together and we have become close friends.
John Madden has also become a good
friend. I also enjoyed appearing on the
Tonight Show with Jay Leno after the Super
Bowl XXX victory. Locally the media has
been pretty cooperative with me, in that

whenever I've asked for some personal
space, they have provided it for me,
which I think is unusual. At times it gets
tough. It's pretty demanding especially
when things are not going real well for
the team, but it has been good. Dallas is
one of the more competitive football mar-
kets for the press with the football team.
So, to be in the middle of that as an athlete
sometimes can be a bit overwhelming, but
I'd rather it be that way than play in a city
where the media and the fans don't care.

As far as the NFL is concerned, I think the game is in pretty good hands.
I would hate to see the league become so corporate oriented that it takes away
from the very fabric of the game. You see it more and more, everything is so money driven.
I'd hate to see it get to the point where they lose sight of the history of the game.
For instance, all the stadiums now have big corporate names on them,
and a lot of the decisions are based on dollars. I understand a certain aspect of that
has to take place but I think sometimes decisions are made for the wrong reasons,
just because of the money that can be generated.

The league, in general, has tried to do everything it can to

protect the quarterbacks.

The problem is, no matter how much they do, unless they
just say: "Hey, you can't hit the quarterbacks,"
the guys are going to get hurt
just because it is a vulnerable position and
it's a physical game. Each year the league tries
to take steps to keep the quarterbacks playing,
but ultimately I don't think it makes
much of a difference.

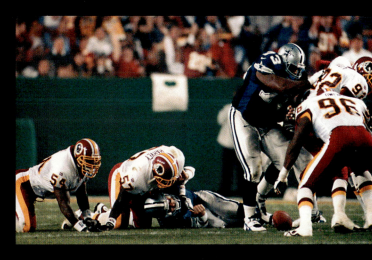

I couldn't imagine the Cowboys ever being as bad as we were in 1989. I knew it couldn't get any worse. I grew up a lot during that year. In the long run, it has made me a better player to go through the season I went through. I've been through tough times, but it has strengthened my character. Earlier this year my house burned down and it is hard to describe what it's like to see your house going up in flames. It was very disappointing, but I tend to view it rather positively. If it had happened a week later, I was going to have every room in the house filled with family members. Right where the electrical fire started was the room where my sister, my brother-in-law and my nephew would have been sleeping. It could have been much worse so I'm just thankful it happened when it did and that no one got injured. The house can be repaired and fixed. It was just something that happened, and that had to be dealt with.

A diagnosis of cancer certainly wakes you up. You realize your own vulnerability and the brevity of life. My mother had gone through a diagnosis of breast cancer the year before, which contributed to us having an appreciation of how precious life is and how temporary some things are. My recently diagnosed cancer and surgery was not quite as dramatic as it might have seemed. I didn't think much of it until I was educated on what could have happened if it hadn't been caught in time. Then I was extremely alarmed, but I was just thankful they were able to take care of it. I certainly did not want to be a poster child for skin cancer, but some people asked if I would be willing to do some public service announcements for it and I did. Through that a lot of people have benefited. I've had a number of people come up to me and say that since they found out that I had it, they had their moles checked. Some of the tests came back malignant, but they were able to catch it early enough. I'm happy other people could benefit from my experience.

I have endured many changes in my life and have learned to use it to my advantage, viewing temporary setbacks as opportunities to grow in new and better ways. Unexpected events in my life led to opportunities that afforded me great success. Embracing inevitable change brought me lasting friendships and professional recognition.

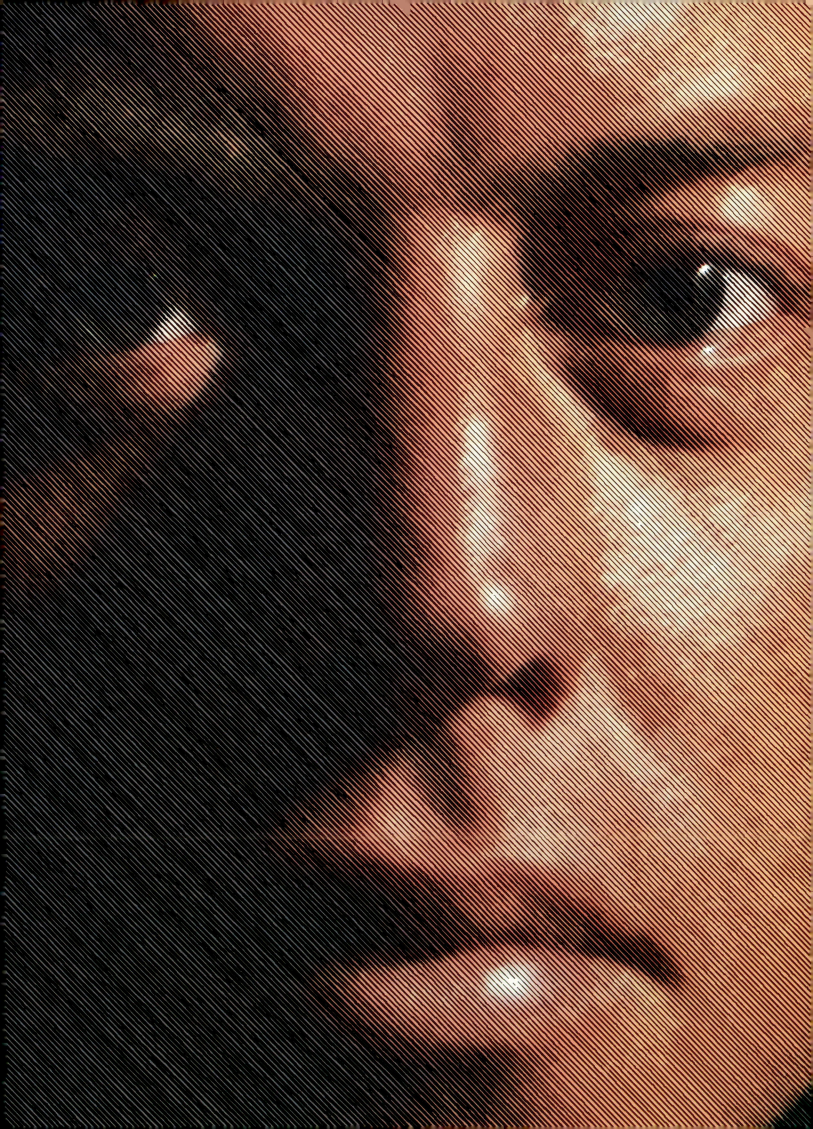

Chapter 3

I don't handle game losses very well, so I'm usually less inclined to be around people after a tough loss. Fortunately, my family and friends have come to realize this over the years and now I don't even hear from them when we lose.

I've had the worst rating of all
NFL quarterbacks and I've been the
Most Valuable Player in the Super Bowl,
so I've been at the bottom
and at the top.

When things don't work out as planned, you can turn defeats into victories by using that disappointment as motivation to work harder. I think having gone through the 1989 season, as painful as it was, really helped me. Each year it makes me realize how fragile success is. It is very hard to win in this league. I was able to discover that my first year with the Cowboys. I've continued to remember that. With each game, with each season that goes by, it keeps me focused and keeps me continually wanting to go out and work and do the things necessary to give me a chance to be successful. Unchanging love of God, my family and friends helps me from being discouraged and keeps me focused in life.

Flaunting my celebrity is not my style. I am what I am. People who see me are either turned on by that or they're not. I can't be all things to all people. I also only do deals with people I feel good about. You can go out (if you're interested in it) and work pretty hard all off-season doing a lot of different deals, small deals and make lots more money. But I really enjoy my

time off. The money is not what drives me. So what I do is pick three, four, five major deals, and just focus my energies on those and do the commitment I have for them and leave the rest alone for the most part.

I have good relationships with those companies I do endorsements for.

For me, it goes beyond, "Here is what we want to pay you and here is what we want you to do." I want to have a relationship with these people. I know the people at Logo Athletic, Coca-Cola and MET-RX. Also I turn down about 90 percent of the offers I receive. I used to hate doing commercials and I just didn't enjoy the photo shoots. I think the reason was my level of expectations wasn't realistic. I thought you can go in and do a commercial in an hour. I'm a believer in regiment and punctuality, but I soon realized that was not the case in television. But over the years, having done a lot of them, I learned to go in with the frame of mind, thinking, 'Hey, this is going to take eight hours,' or however long you're going to be there. So now, I've begun to enjoy the process more.

The important thing to realize, and I think a lot of players fail to realize this, is **no one wants you to endorse a product for them just because they think you're a nice guy.** Any activities or involvements you might have in the off-season that help you earn extra money, they are all dependent on how we do as a football team. And I've never lost sight of it. So I don't ever get to the point where I'm doing things that take away from my game preparations. Once we're not doing well on the football field, all that will stop, **believe me.**

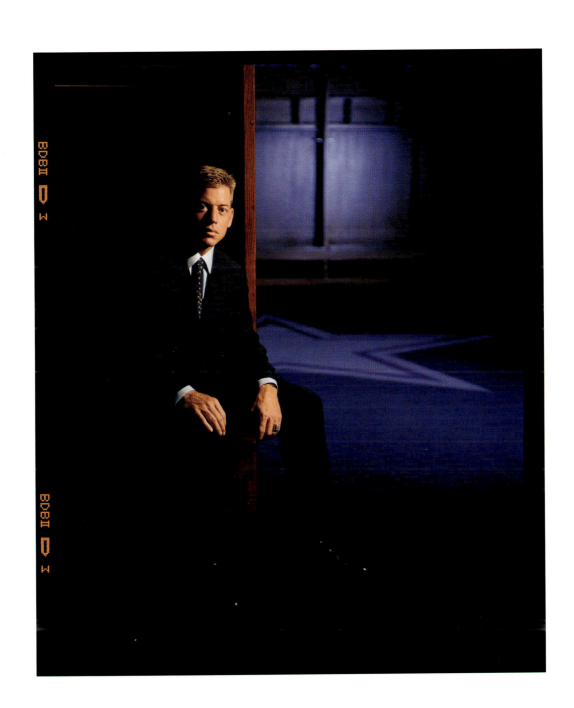

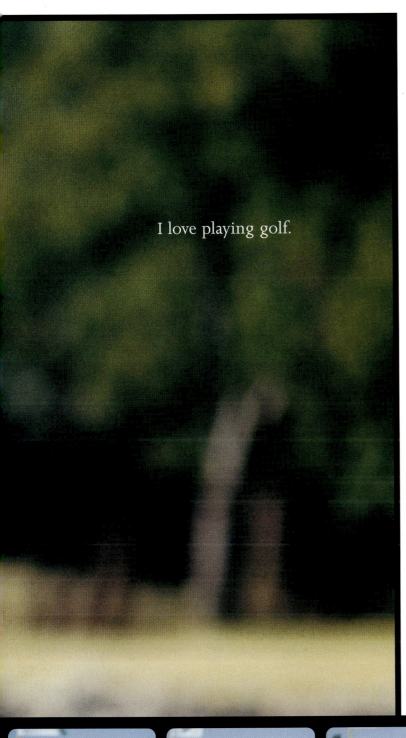

I love playing golf.

I picked up the game avidly about four years ago and I play every chance I get in the off-season. I don't get to play much during the season. Most of the vacations and trips that I plan during the off-season are centered around golf and usually the beach. I love the ocean, so I tend to spend my vacation time in warm, tropical climates, where golf courses are plentiful. My handicap gets down to about 10 during the off-season, and I look forward to dedicating myself to playing a lot more when I'm not playing football anymore. But heavens no, I won't become a pro. I would love to, but I'm not good enough. I've come close to having a hole-in-one, but I've never had one. The other day in Wichita Falls, we had a Miller Lite-sponsored golf tournament and a 67-year-old neurosurgeon got a hole-in-one. It was amazing.

I like country music

and over the years I have become friends with a
number of recording artists such as Toby Keith
on NFL album projects, but I thought that
I would give my voice, as well as the listening public, a break
and not record another album.
Race car driving is also one of my passions. It gives me a great rush of
freedom and escapism. I don't know how the coaching staff
would feel if it knew about my racing.

I grew up riding motorcycles in Oklahoma
and I always had entertained the idea of getting a Harley.

About a year and a half ago, Barry Switzer asked me whether I would be interested in getting a Harley. It was funny because just the day before I passed by a Harley store and mentioned to a friend of mine: 'Boy, I always wanted to get a Harley. One of these days I'm going to get one.' The very next day Barry came to me and said: 'Hey, have you ever had any interest in getting a Harley? I have an opportunity to get one, and if you're interested I can get one for you too.'

That's how I got one and I just love the feeling of freedom riding my Harley.

We don't have a lot of free time during road trips, unlike some of the other sports. I normally just relax in the hotel, and try to get some rest. Normally we get checked in the hotels and get enough time to get situated, then we're off to meetings and dinner, then we're back in our rooms for a bit of time relaxing and watching movies. In the morning we're up for a pre-game meal and as soon as that's over, we're on a bus off to the stadium to get ready for the game. We don't have a lot of down time in the cities when we're on the road. Normally they have tight security at the hotels where we're staying.

In 1992, I established the Troy Aikman Foundation to benefit disadvantaged children in the Dallas-Fort Worth area. My mom, Charlyn, along with the Board of Directors, runs the foundation. My mom pretty much handles all the day-to-day activities concerning the foundation. She really enjoys being involved. At this time we have funded three Aikman's End Zones; one at Cook Children's Medical Center

in Fort Worth, one at Children's Medical Center of Dallas and one at Children's Hospital in Oklahoma. In Aikman's End Zone we hope to inspire hospitalized children to come together by providing

them with tools to help them learn, imagine and dream. Through modern technology these kids have the opportunity to travel beyond ordinary boundaries, see new places, meet new people and explore worlds most kids would think unimaginable. I can't think of a more useful, inspiring application of high-tech interactivity than to help battle the isolation and challenges that hospitalized kids face. The kids just love

the visual imagery and virtual reality in the kid-friendly, football-themed playrooms. I find this project very rewarding, and we are working at expanding the concept to other areas.

We partnered with Steven Spielberg's Starbright Foundation to improve the lives of seriously ill children and their families. Starbright is a collaboration of pediatric health-care professionals, technology experts and leaders in the entertainment field. Our goal is to develop new tools and programs to empower ill children to deal with their challenges such as pain, stress, isolation, fear, anxiety and low self-esteem. We never forget the child behind the illness and work with the kids in finding answers and solutions. The founda-

tion board, as well as myself, became frustrated until we teamed up with Starbright because we received many corporate dollars, but we were not able to get them out to the kids like we thought we would be able to. Once we decided to do the interactive playrooms, we could see exactly what the money was being used for, we could see the benefits for the kids. It is almost as rewarding for me and for my board and for those people involved corporately as it is for the kids.

Aikman Family 1996

from left to right

Mike Powell, Tammy Powell(sister), Terri Starns(sister), David Starns,

Troy Aikman, Brooke Foreman(niece),

Drew Powell(nephew), Brady Foreman(nephew)

I make time to spend with my family and friends.

During the season I don't get to spend as much time with family or friends as I would have liked to but during the off-season I spend my vacation time with family and friends. I see my family regularly. My mother and oldest sister live in the Dallas area and my other sister attends all our home games during the year. **My family is very close and I try to see my niece and nephews as often as possible. I love kids and would like to get married and have a family of my own one day.** I've always wanted four kids, but at the rate I'm going that might be a reach. I would be happy with two, but I've always wanted a big family of boys or girls. People nowadays are having kids at later ages, and that's fine by me.

I'm very much looking forward to that aspect of my life when it happens, but in the meantime I'm very happy and content with my life as it is. People may say: 'Ah, here's this guy who is alone, and he is lonely', but that's not true, I'm very happy. People often think that, if they only had such or such. If they can only find this person, have this new car or house or achieve that on the corporate ladder, they will be happy, but I think that if you are not happy with yourself, it doesn't matter what you get, you will not be happy. No one or no thing is going to make you happy, you have to find happiness within yourself.

I have strong faith in God. I used to be actively involved and often spoke in churches when I was in college in Oklahoma. The older I've gotten, my faith has become more of a personal relationship for me. I don't talk a lot about it, some do, and that's fine. For me, faith is more of a personal thing, but it is something that is extremely important

to me. I do believe in heaven and in hell, and I don't think any of us can truly comprehend what heaven will be like. Obviously it's a place that's better than anything that any of us ever experienced here. I look forward to seeing what heaven is like.

I'm really not certain
how many more years I'll play.
I've always said that as long as I'm enjoying myself
I will continue to play.

You give of yourself too much for an eight-month period to not enjoy what you're doing. I would like to play for another five or six years, or until I can't play anymore. I don't see myself getting into coaching when I finish my playing career. I would like, however, to stay involved in football in some capacity. I would entertain the idea of getting involved in the front office. I'd be interested in having an ownership role in a club. Fortunately it's not a big concern of mine, as far as what I'm going to be doing when my playing days are over. I'm keeping my options open. I don't want to get so isolated into one thing that I don't have the flexibility of doing what I want to do. Throughout my career I've

met a lot of neat people and I'm confident that when I'm done playing football some things will materialize that will keep me interested, and keep me motivated. I realize that I can't just play golf every day, I'd get bored with it. You can't get stagnant. It's not about making money, it's about keeping yourself energized. It's about having goals.

I always look forward. I never look back and think what could have been. Some of the biggest setbacks in my life have inspired me the most to reach greater heights. I've enjoyed the aging process, to learn and grow. I've learned a lot more about what's important to me and what my priorities are. I try to keep my expectations realistic and look to the future with realistic optimism.

I would like to be remembered as a great quarterback, but more importantly, I would like to be remembered as a guy who gave great effort and did everything he could to help his team win and was respected by his teammates.